STARTERS
LONG AGO
BOOK

North American Indians

Macdonald Educational

Long ago these Indians lived in North America.
They lived in a village.
They hunted and farmed.
2

North American Indians lived in groups
called tribes.
Tribes in each part of the country
had their own way of living.

This is a tribe of travelling Indians.
They lived in tents called tepees.
The tents were made from buffalo skins
and could be carried easily.

4

maize

Some Indian tribes travelled
to find food.
Other tribes were farmers.
The women often did the work in the fields.

Indian men were hunters.
These men are catching fish.
They caught the fish with spears.

6

spear

Sometimes Indians hunted alligators.
They found them in the swamps.

bow and arrow

Long ago, Indians had no horses.
They hunted on foot.
They moved quietly.
These hunters are trying to surround a stag.

Later, Indians hunted on horseback.
They usually hunted buffalo.
They chased herds of buffalo
and killed as many as they could eat.

skin tepee

cleaning skin

painting skin

sewing skin

Buffaloes were important to Indians.
The Indians ate the meat.
They made clothes and tepees with the skins.
Sometimes they painted the skins.
10

loom

basket

Indian women made all the clothes.
Some Indians wove cloth on looms.
They wove rugs and blankets too.

beadwork

These Indians used feathers and beads
to decorate their clothes and headdresses.
12

Here are some Indian totem poles.
Totem poles were carved and painted.
The pictures told a kind of story
about the tribe.

These Indians are doing a buffalo dance.
They danced round a fire.
They hoped it would make them good hunters.

14

Other Indian tribes had war dances.
They danced before a battle
to bring them luck.

15

Some Indian tribes used smoke signals
for sending very simple messages.
16

wampum beads

Wampum beads were woven into patterns.
They were used as money.

settlers' ship

Indian canoe

White people came from Europe
to live in America.
At first the Indians were friendly.
They sold goods to the settlers.

Later the Indians became angry
with the settlers.
Sometimes they attacked their camps.

These Indians are on the Trail of Tears.
They are going to find a new home.
They are sad about leaving their own village.
20

Here is an Indian warrior.
His headdress shows he is a chief.
He is going to war.

The cavalry were mounted soldiers.
They protected white settlers.
The cavalry fought many battles
with the Indians.

The battles were very fierce.
The cavalry had guns.
Sometimes the Indians had guns too.
Many people were killed.

The Indians and the settlers
often tried to make peace.
They had many meetings.
Sometimes they smoked the pipe of peace.

Now there are only a few Indians
in America.
Most of them live in special camps
called reservations.

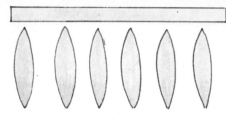

See if you can make
a feather headdress.
You can make it out of paper.
Paint it in bright colours.

Try modelling a totem pole
in clay.
Paint it when the clay is dry.

Index

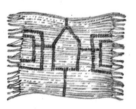